W9-CLU-489

In memory of Thelma Lambert

~A.M.

For Mom and Dad

~J.M.

First American edition published in 1998 by
Crocodile Books, USA
An imprint of Interlink Publishing Group, Inc.
99 Seventh Avenue, Brooklyn, New York 11215
Text © by Anne Mangan 1998
Illustrations © by Joanne Moss 1998
Published simultaneously in Great Britain by Magi Publications
Library of Congress Cataloging-in-Publication Data
Mangan, Anne, 1942-
The smallest bear / by Anne Mangan ; illustrated by Joanne Moss.
– 1st American ed.   p.   cm.
Summary: Browny, the smallest bear in the Big Wood, is too small to reach
the honey that will help him grow and worries that he will never get bigger.
ISBN 1-56656-266-X
[1. Bears–Fiction. 2. Size–Fiction.]   I. Moss, Joanne, 1971- ill. II. Title.
PZ7.M3126425Br 1998 [E]–dc21 97-29669 CIP AC
All rights reserved.
Printed and bound in Belgium
10 9 8 7 6 5 4 3 2 1

The Smallest ~Bear~

by Anne Mangan

illustrated by Joanne Moss

Crocodile Books, USA

An imprint of Interlink Publishing Group, Inc.
NEW YORK

FRANKLIN PIERCE
COLLEGE LIBRARY
RINDGE, N.H. 0346.

Browny was the smallest of all the bears that lived in the Big Wood. He grew so slowly that it seemed as if he did not grow at all. The other young bears would roll him on the ground and play roly-poly with him, and often they would tease him. "You need to eat more honey," they laughed, "so that you will grow bigger."

One day Browny licked Mother Bear's face.
"Yum, you taste nice," he said.
"It must be the honey I ate," said Mother Bear.
"Can you get some for me so I can grow bigger?"
"No, Browny," said Mother Bear. "Every bear
must find his own honey. It is the law of the
Big Wood."

Browny ambled off into the Wood. There he
saw some young bears gathered around a tree
where bees were buzzing.
"Please may I have some of your honey?"
he asked them, "so I can grow bigger?"
"This is *our* honey," said the big bears. "Go and
find your own!"
And they growled at him and chased him away.

Browny wandered on. Suddenly he came
across his Uncle Bruin, who had one paw
down a hole in a treetrunk.
"Is that honey in there, Uncle Bruin?"
asked Browny. "Please may I have some
so I can grow bigger?"
"No, you may not," replied Uncle Bruin.
"Every bear must find his own honey.
It is the law of the Big Wood. Surely your
mother told you that?"

Browny felt sad. Uncle Bruin was usually so kind. Browny cheered up, though, when he saw his own friends.

"We're going to look for honey," they called.

"Ooh," said Browny. "I'd like that. I want to grow bigger, you see. May I come, too?"

"No," said the bears. "You're much too small to reach the bees' nests."

Browny didn't know what to do. He couldn't grow bigger if he didn't eat honey, and he couldn't eat honey because he wasn't big enough to climb trees!

Just at that moment, along came Mr. Moose.
He was another friend, and he was BIG.
Surely he must know how to grow without
eating honey?
"How can I be as big as you?" asked Browny.
"Some of us are big and some are little," said
Mr. Moose, and without saying another
word he strode on, with his antlers
touching the branches of the trees.
"Well, *that's* not much help," said
Browny to himself.

Browny walked on till he reached the lake.
He stood in the water and watched the fish
swimming and splashing. Perhaps *they* would
know how he could grow bigger?
"We only grow as big as we are meant to be,"
said a little fish. "You have to wait to grow."
"But I want to grow *now*!" cried the little bear,
splashing angrily out of the water.

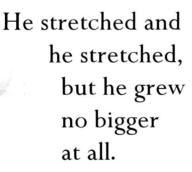

Browny stood under
a tree by the shore
and, taking hold of
one of the lowest
branches, he began
to stretch himself.
"This will make me
grow a bit bigger.
Then I'll be able to get some honey and grow
bigger still," he said to himself.
He stretched and
he stretched,
but he grew
no bigger
at all.

"You do look funny,"
cried a voice above
his head.

"Don't let your friends
see you. They will only laugh." It was Squirrel.
What friends? Browny sat up and there, coming
towards him, were the big young bears
who had growled and chased him
earlier in the day.

"They'll think I'm after their honey again," cried
Browny. "Oh, where can I hide?"
"There, over there!" said Squirrel, and Browny
saw some large tree roots arching up over the
ground. He was just small enough to squeeze
between them.
"Aren't you glad now you didn't
grow when you stretched?"
Squirrel called
after him.

Browny pushed his way through roots and branches, through briars and tall weeds.
All of a sudden, he came out into a clearing with a lake in the middle.
The sun shone between the trees, and there were butterflies and ladybugs and dragonflies and bees.
And where there are bees, there is *honey!*

The bees kept their honey in a tiny hole
between tree roots, just big enough for
Browny's little paws. He scooped
some out and he ate and . . .

. . . he ate till he could eat no more.
Then he stretched out in a patch of sunlight
and fell fast asleep.

When Browny woke up, he wandered over
to the lake and looked at himself in the water.
He was still as small as ever, but suddenly
it didn't seem to matter any more.
He didn't need to be big to get honey.
He didn't need to be big to be happy.
He was all right—just the way he was!

FRANKLIN PIERCE COLLEGE LIBRARY

00117304